A Pig in a Wig

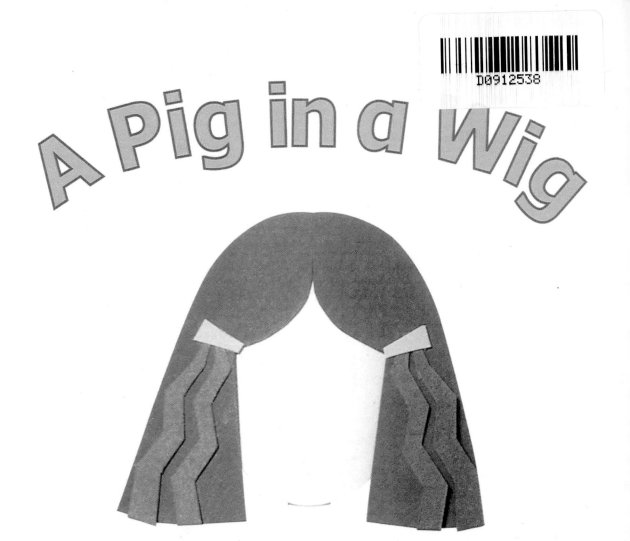

Written by Elizabeth Apgar

Illustrated by Sally Vitsky

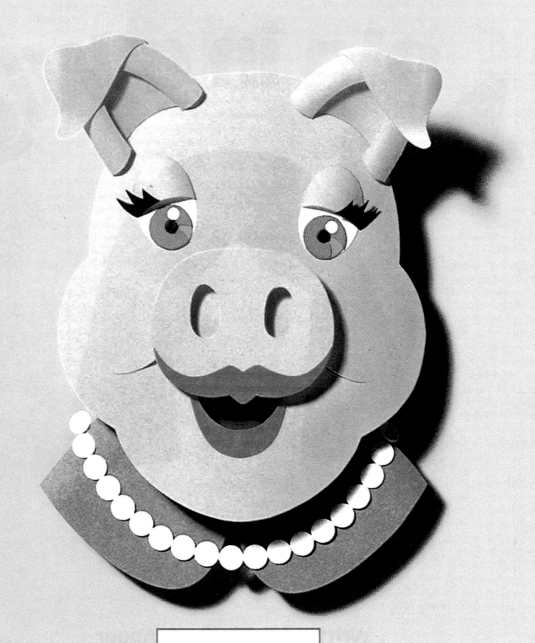

A pig.

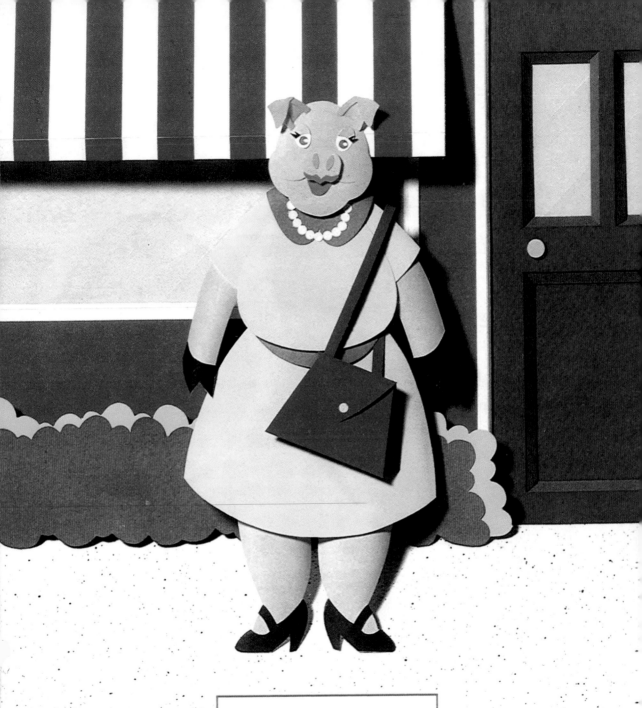

A big pig.

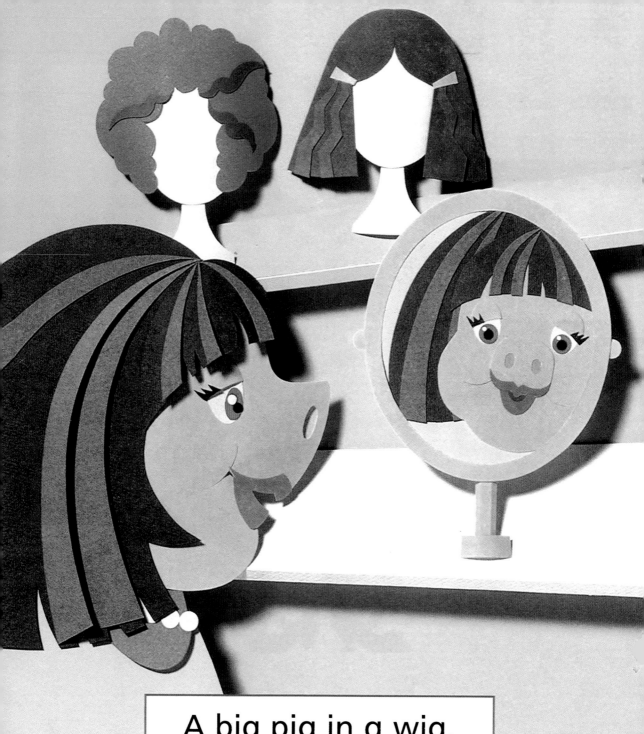

A big pig in a wig.

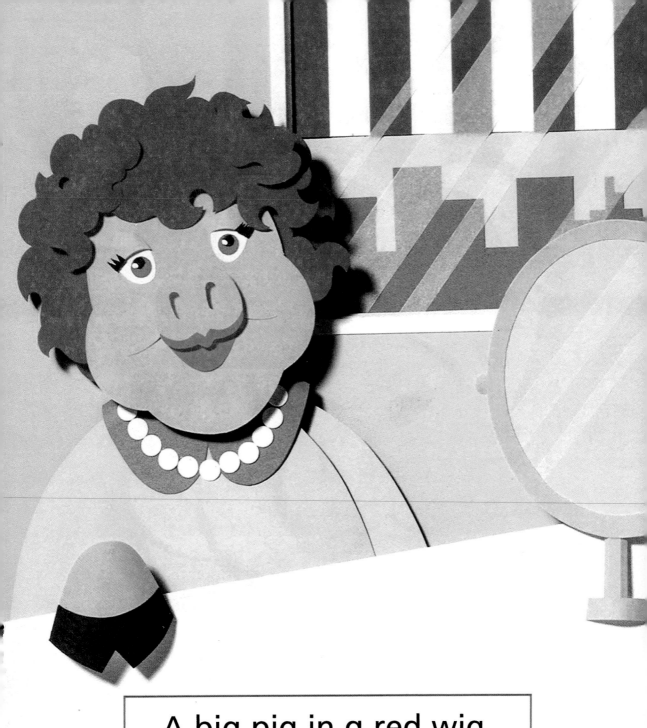

A big pig in a red wig.

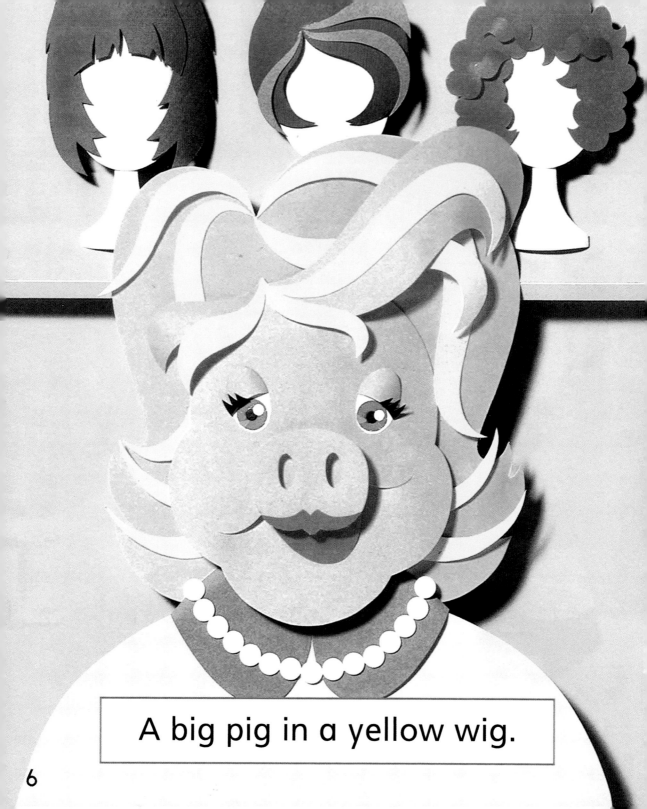

A big pig in a yellow wig.

6

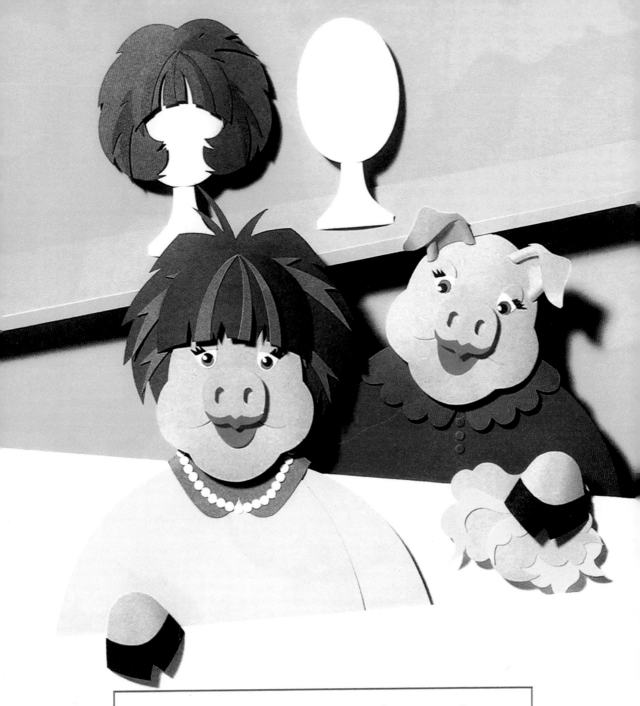

A big pig in a blue wig.

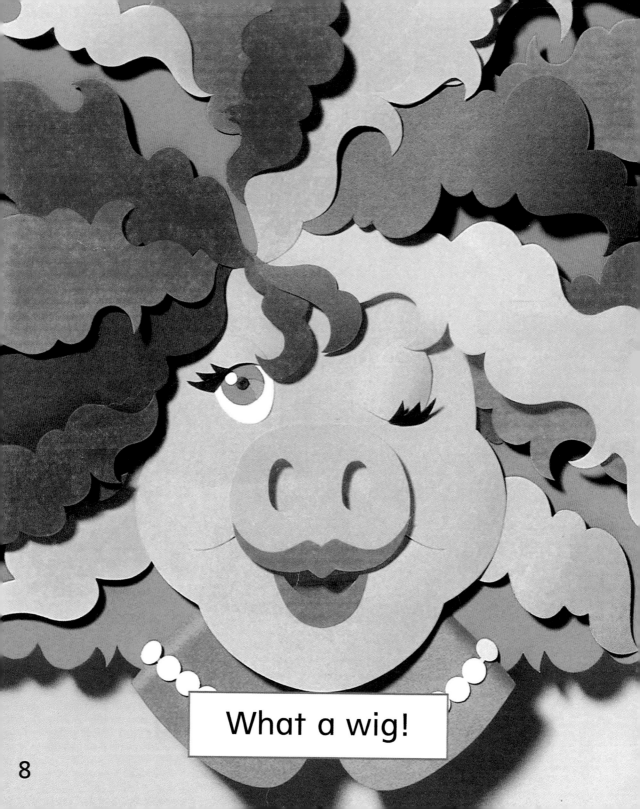

What a wig!